Best Gift Ideas For Women

Perfect Gifts Ideas For Any Special Occasion

Taylor Timms

> **Author Online!**
> For updates and free women seduction tips visit Taylor Timms page at
>
> **www.foreverlaid.com**

Best Gift Ideas For Women :
Perfect Gifts Ideas For Any Special Occasion
by **Taylor Timms**

ISBN 978-0-9866004-4-9

Printed in the United States of America

Copyright © 2010 Psylon Press

All rights reserved. Except for use in a review, no portion of this book may be reproduced in any form without the express written permission of the author. For information regarding permission, write to Apartado 0426-01559, David, Chiriqui, Panama

Neither the author nor the publisher assumes any responsibility for the use or misuse of information contained in this book.

Also by Taylor Timms

Forever Laid Formula
Best Ways To Get Women To Sleep With You
ISBN 978-0-9866004-2-5

Free Online Seduction Course

As a thank you for buying this book, I would like to give you free access to my online women seduction course.

To claim your free spot, please go to

www.foreverlaid.com

and enter your valid email address now. There are only a limited number of spots available – we may be forced to close the doors soon.

CONTENTS

1. Introduction	2
2. What gifts do women really want?	7
3. Gift giving rules	16
4. Flowers, beautiful flowers	25
5. How you can go really wrong	33
6. Be unpredictable!	47
7. On chocolates	52
8. ...And diamonds	57
9. How desperate are you?	62
10. A few really good ideas	71
11. Special occasions	78
Appendix	87

INTRODUCTION

Ah, women. They make the highs higher and the lows more frequent.

(Friedrich W. Nietzshe)

By buying this book, you are giving yourself an invaluable gift on the wisdom and importance of giving women gifts and by following these guidelines and suggested ideas, you are sure to come out a winner every time. You have chosen wisely by selecting this book.

Giving a woman a gift is fast becoming a studied art. It is no easy feat impressing a woman nowadays, but here are some really useful and God sent ideas and suggestions on how you can win the heart of a lady without doing too many cartwheels and still be appreciated for a long time afterwards.

When you go out of your way, you go out and about, you make the time and effort to go to stores and spend time picking out something special just for her, to choose a gift you think she will really like, well, then you are one lucky person: you will be appreciated, regarded with more respect, affection and even loved all that much more.

There is no greater warmth, no greater appreciation, love, gratitude and feelings of overwhelming tenderness than when a woman receives a gift. This, when she is least expecting it. Even on occasions when she is expecting it, like her birthday (woe is you should you forget that date.)

You might have heard this a hundred times before, from friends, your sisters, your mothers and aunts – but yes, women *do* love receiving gifts. If any woman ever says otherwise, she's lying through her teeth.

There is just something really terrific when a man really does invest all that energy into buying a gift for her. It symbolizes his feelings, it demonstrates his thoughtfulness to her – saying that he cares, that he is thinking of her and that gesture means the whole world to her.

It's a physical demonstration of affection and consideration on a woman's level and she will appreciate the time and energy you invest in this thoughtful act; which in turn, will also make you feel appreciated. That is a pretty good way to feel after seeing her reaction to her gift. It's a win-win situation.

A woman realizes that a man is paying attention to either the things she's saying, like little things she's said in the past that she liked or the things she surrounds herself with, even a certain pastime of hers. She is made aware that you put some serious thinking into it, no matter how spontaneous the gesture is.

And she *loves* it.

The whole gift giving act is one of sheer enjoyment, the wrapped-up surprise, the unexpected thoughtfulness or even when it is expected, it's lovely that you went the extra mile for her.

And giving women gifts is all about going the extra mile for them. Try and not buy a woman a gift – at all – ever; then I'd like to see where that would get you…

A woman will somehow always sense when a man takes extra care in getting her a gift that is special, rather than just slapping something together hurriedly and forcing a guilty smile as if it really *is* special when it isn't. Don't make that mistake. A woman's intuition is just that perceptive.

A special gift *will* have that magical power to make her feel special and that in itself will send out a chain work of all nice goodies following it.

And it does not necessarily have to be ridiculously expensive. It isn't about the money – it's about the *thoughtfulness.*

Giving a gift to a woman really does make her feel loved; even if it's that hardened work colleague of yours who never smiles. She's smiling on the inside and believe it or not, you have cracked the ice. Well, at least started melting some of it.

Even in a long term relationship, the power of gift giving should never be undermined. On anniversaries, birthdays and all the other special days throughout the year, a man should *always* give his partner, his mom or his sister a gift. It solidifies the bonds, creates deeper roots of love and cements relationships that might seem to be weakening. It might not mend broken bridges but it certainly can build a new tentative one. Even when a couple or siblings have argued and things are tense in a relationship, giving a gift you chose yourself and carefully picked it out can erase the tension and bring in the relief of forgiveness. It is here that buying a gift for a woman can almost manifest miracles. If it doesn't, then it comes pretty close.

WHAT GIFTS DO WOMEN *REALLY* WANT?

If women didn't exist, all the money in the world would have no meaning.

(Aristotle Onassis)

Inspiration.

That elusive muse that sometimes fails when you need it the most.

Trying to work out what it is that women want for their birthday, for Christmas, for their anniversary can be quite tough if you have not done your homework. Not listened to the little things she has said in the past or paid any attention whatsoever to her likes or decorations...

And when inspiration fails, here are some real answers from real women, girls and ladies to help you get inspired as to what you should buy a woman because it is exactly what she wants. It might be the very thing she will not buy for herself – that happens more often than not. So it is here that you step in and make yourself stand out shiningly from the crowd.

The very one gift a woman would most love in the whole wide world is:

Wait for it…

It might be the last thing you're expecting out of this dame of yours:

Travel.

There is no gift more luscious or thrilling as giving a woman the gift of a getaway from the home environment. It does not necessarily have to be an expensive vacation in Paris, although that would certainly put the sparkle in her eye! It could even be a day retreat at a beauty spa - this one is always a winner; the gift of pampering a woman is always welcome!

It could even be a weekend away to any destination in the country, be it a city escape or the quiet countryside. Or a cruise. Or a packaged tour. Or mini vacation to the nearest seaside town. It doesn't matter where it is, as long as *it is.*

You'd certainly not take her to the snake park if she was terrified of snakes! Some basic common sense should be present here.

Although it might surprise a man to hear this, the gift of a trip can be a truly Heaven sent gift, just right to captivate a lady's heart, or whatever else it is you're trying to captivate.

Funnily enough, if a man were asked for his ideal gift – I think it would be more along the lines of a new electronic gadget just out on the market; a new computer, a new car or even a new digital camera. "Boys with toys…"

The idea of getting away, whether it is for a day or a couple of weeks is so desired that when it cannot be obtained as a gift, a woman *will* go out and get this gift for herself. And why?

Today's world is so demanding on women, what with careers, family life and responsibilities of living both lives. It can get really hard, so the thought of getting away is really a tempting one. It relieves stress. It eases those responsibilities. It stops the crazy juggling for a very brief period of time. Whether a woman is a mother with kids or just a career girl – it is a dog eat dog world and women are part of the competitive struggle to be better and achieve more.

This is the number one gift a man could possible offer any woman-: the opportunity to unwind and relax or to just get away for an exciting adventure. You'll just have to take a rain check on that laptop for the time being…

Based on a recent survey done on over a thousand American adults, other gift choices came up that seemed pretty important to women as well, besides travel or a getaway, which rated as the best gifts a woman could receive.

Flowers.

This is one gift women really enjoy receiving, regardless of age or occasion. They are always welcome, more so when they are given with meaning. It has become so popular, so world wide used but it is still a lovely gift to receive. Especially from a loved one. Even if it isn't an actual arrangement, it can even be a single rose or a plant, potted or flowering plant; it is still very much appreciated to receive. With a flower arrangement, if she really likes the flowers, if the occasion is a really special one or if it's you who is the really special person – she can have her flowers dried and they can remain for posterity to remind her of its special significance.

Jewelry.

You gentlemen have always known about this one. It's even the favorite gift men really like buying a woman. Jewelry can be a lavish gift of luxury and value, depending on your income. Or it can be a simple symbolic gift that is eternal.

It does not have to be wildly expensive trinket that you cannot afford; women might see that as extravagance and suspect you're a squanderer… or just take the gift to later bye-bye to you when you're broke. But jewelry is always appreciated, especially if it carries some value and is not cheap looking imitations… Taste is essential here. **Her** taste.

Books.

Another very welcome gift. It's always a good idea to know a woman's tastes in books. It can be about a hobby of hers or just plain romance novels. There's always a book to suit different tastes. You certainly wouldn't give a cookery book to your beloved on Valentine's Day over a romantic dinner… Just as you wouldn't give a book on dating techniques to your grandparents, as a general rule, either.

Giving a book as a gift to a woman has to suit her lifestyle, be in accordance with her interests and likes and for that, a little bit of investigative work could be handy.

Even if it's your single great-aunt who has 101 cats; she'll still appreciate a new book on her favorite subject: Cats.

Clothes.

This gift can get tricky.

If there's an item you know she has been wanting for some time; go right ahead and buy it for her. It'll be really appreciated and she really will really love you for it. However, if you aren't 100% sure of what kinds of clothes she likes… You aren't sure of her size and if you two are still getting to know each other

– then you stay away from clothes as a gift.

Women usually know what they like and they know exactly what they want in clothes. It can be a relationship killer if you give her (what *you* think) is a gorgeous pair of jeans and she secretly thinks that the style makes her hips look twice as wide…

The whole exchanging of gifts can sometimes be hurtful rather than delightful. It isn't because you're insensitive; on the contrary – it *is* because you care and have put quite some thought into this gift giving experience that you're pretty sure that the gift you'll give will be a wonderful experience.

Not true. Well, not always.

A friend of mine told me about her gift receiving experience of an ex-boyfriend of hers.

They had been together for a year when they decided to celebrate their 1st anniversary at home alone over a romantic candlelit dinner. She'd made him his favorite dish, got all dressed up and was really expecting romance.

When he arrived home, slightly late, he was really irritated that he'd got stuck in the rain, he'd had to stop at the corner store to buy her a box of chocolates and he hadn't been able to get a parking spot, he'd gotten soaked through and he'd gotten the car all dirty.

He'd had a nightmare of a day at work, his boss had been on his case all day and he'd come really close to quitting.

These things do tend happen at the worst timings.

He didn't give her the gift; he had just put it on the table. He didn't even apologize for being late. After all, he'd just been through hell.

But he did remember their anniversary and he was happy about their evening together.

She told him that he needn't have gone through so much trouble just to buy her a gift. That there had never been any obligation for him to do so. He didn't get that.

It was later that she told me how furious she felt that the gift, the occasion and his attitude had all been because he felt obliged. He didn't get her the symbolic gift of a one year anniversary; he got damned angry only.

It is not about *having* to give a woman a gift; it's about really *wanting* to. It's about going up to her and presenting her with that special something. Or if it's a surprise gift – it really *is* about finding that unexpected package hidden under her quilt, while you secretly watch. A woman knows when you really mean it. She sure doesn't want you to catch pneumonia because of it – although she might think it is sweet that you didn't mind catching it just because getting her that gift and seeing that lovely smile was all worth it…

GIFT GIVING RULES

Be to her virtues very kind; be to her faults a little blind.

(Matthew Prior)

Whether you're a man or a woman, you, like everybody, have gone through the torture of trying to find the exact perfect gift for a partner and been at a total loss as to what to get.

Not the generic gift that you can give to just about anyone; *the* perfect gift. The kind that has her gasping with pleasure, eyes shining like stars, where she nearly jumps on you in sheer exhilaration.

This is the one reaction which is the most gratifying and whoever can evoke this reaction from a simple gift is truly a hero! Even if you're one temporarily only.

It isn't always easy to buy a woman the one gift you know she would be thrilled to receive. You might go to all the malls, listen to what saleswomen have to say, they sometimes are the best people to consult - after all - they're women, too. You might pop into all kinds of gift stores, search for ideas in catalogs as well.

Still, inspiration might fail you. In the end, you'll just buy something, either because you're running out of time or you're just plain tired. And what you end up buying really does seem like a gorgeous gift. But turns out to be less than mediocre.

Online, there are thousands of sites giving you advice on buying gifts for women. The majority of them are just advertisements for your run-of-the-mill products that have no unique meaning and by the time you have actually filtered one or two gifts that you think would be ideal, hours have flown by.

This chapter is aimed at providing you with a brief guide of buying gifts. For women as well as men. Because tastes are so varied, what women most desire is not the same as what men are keen on. A gift you would give a woman is not the same as you would give a man. Well, in some instances, anyway.

Women's preferences and individual tastes are vastly different from those of men's.

So this guide is the summary of hundreds of men and women's ideas on their ideal gifts.

It aims at simplifying the basic rules on what to offer as a gift to someone you care about. It helps you out when that streak of inspiration fails you.

It is, basically, the only guide you'll ever need in a nutshell.

This guide actually deserves a whole book dedicated to it as there are so many different ideas that women have given as perfect gifts. Men have supplied their own ideas of their ideal gifts – and there really are too many; it would be too confusing.

So, combining some basic common sense with a little creativity into a practical, accessible guide; narrowing down the main ideas into a few rules that make it palatable and really helpful for the reader – these rules came to fruition. One set suited for men. One for women.

Note: This is a basic guide only. The rules suggested here can be adapted to any budget and occasion. The whole idea of providing this guide really is to aim at that exhilarated reaction of a loved one when you get that outstanding gift. And good luck to you – you will sure have gained points by following these rules.

THE 4 RULES FOR GIVING WOMEN GIFTS

1. One of the best gifts you can give a woman is one that is simply for luxury. To spoil her. It has no practical use. For example, a mini vacation, her favorite perfume, jewelry, a book, candy, clothing or accessories, a day at a spa, a tasteful decorative trinket or flowers.

Gifts that men would have no functional use for. These are ideal gifts women love.

There it is. As simple as that.

2. Let's imagine that she needs a new appliance. Or she happens to mention that she'd really like a new gadget, like a digital camera or other electrical appliance. It could even be a new dishwasher or tumble drier.

So, you decide to wow her with a *practical* gift. Then you buy the better version. The luxury model. The attractive one. Or the one that has more functions to make her life easier.

3. Avoid:

Weight loss programs, supplements or books.

Anti wrinkle creams or treatments.

Hair removal creams or equipment.

Any appliance that is for housework, e.g., a vacuum cleaner.

Self improvement books.

4. Out of the blue – surprise her with a flower. Or 20 – an arrangement.

For no apparent reason, buy her flowers. Not because it's her birthday nor because you had an argument, just because you care.

This gesture is a winner every time.

Women always appreciate the time a make makes to go out of his way. Especially to buy her a gift. It's incredible, but women go for quality rather than quantity in gifts. It's better to give her a small gift she truly enjoys rather than a large gift which she'll put to one side. However, the gesture of giving her small little trinkets or luxuries is just as welcome. It's all about your thoughtfulness. The fact that you invested the time and money goes down really well in her books. There is no greater feeling in the world as feeling cherished and that is what giving women gifts does: it makes them feel loved and warm and treasured.

THE 4 RULES FOR GIVING MEN GIFTS:

1. A really good gift for a man is one that he can put to good use. One that is practical. That he can fiddle with. That he can spend a couple of hours working on it.

It can be related to a hobby of his, golf or horse riding. It can be an electronic gadget – that really is an all time favorite! A GPS system, laptop or car DVD system, for example.

2. If a woman asks a man what he would like for Christmas or for his birthday, he *will* tell her. She should ask him directly, when out shopping or browsing. Men don't usually drop hints about their gift preferences. In that regard, they are openly candid. A woman can just go on out and buy it, she doesn't even have to get too creative about it.

3. Nowadays, more and more men are really starting to look after themselves: going to parlors for manicures, pedicures, hair stylists, clothes stylists, waxing and even eyebrow shaping.

Yes, some of them really are.

If a man enjoys any of these, it's a wonderful treat if she can make an appointment for him for an Indian head massage or full body massage.

This gift is *only* if he likes this sort of pampering.

4. Another suggested gift is her permission.

Strange as it may sound, but a really good gift could be her suggesting that he has a night out with his friends or a golfing day out with the boys.

If he's surprised by this kind of gift, she should tell him that it's her way of showing him how much she cares; it doesn't always have to be time spent with her.

It really isn't all that difficult to please a man or impress him. On the whole, though, the majority of men do enjoy practical gifts especially gift that has him entertained for a while. An electrical appliance that he's had his eye on or a gismo that is related to his hobby, whether it's fishing or flying lessons. When a woman gives a man a toy to tinker with for a few hours, she will see how much he will really appreciate her consideration.

FLOWERS, BEAUTIFUL FLOWERS

Bread feeds the body; indeed, but flowers feed also the soul.

(The Koran)

Here's the secret about giving flowers as a gift:

They are more appreciated and enjoyed when they come unexpectedly and for no special reason except to demonstrate that you are thinking about her.

It really is a fact that women absolutely love receiving flowers when they're given as a surprise. And this doesn't apply to romantic situations exclusively. It can be given to a relative, a sibling, a work colleague or just a friend. But when it does come from your partner, it is more valuable and cherished.

Because it comes unexpectedly, it is even lovelier, nicer and warmer. All women will agree here.

Giving a bunch of roses or an arrangement of mixed flowers should always be given according to taste. The majority of women prefer mixed flowers; this is typical for other relationships that are not the romantic kind.

Roses, on the other hand, have always been and will always be the favorite flower for the language of love. Or any other desired romantic involvement.

You will most commonly see red roses on romantic occasions, like Valentine's Day. But women don't mind receiving *any* color roses when they're sprung on her as a surprise. Red will always be the traditional color for love, though.

As this is a book for giving women gifts, it is only right to include a guide on giving women flowers.

These tips and suggestions are to help a man when it comes to buying flowers for a woman.

A FEW TIPS:

- **Flowers ≠ marriage**

If you're hesitant about offering a woman flowers or you think it's really early in your acquaintanceship to be offering flowers, it really *is* okay. A woman will see the gesture for exactly what it is: a gesture of consideration, friendliness or thoughtfulness.

Even red roses usually convey romance; not necessarily commitment, and a woman will have enough intuition to know that.

- **Flowers for all ages**

So you'll give flowers to your loved one. On special occasions and, better yet, just because you want her to know you love her, on an ordinary day.

But flowers say so much to *all* women and girls.

A mother loves receiving flowers from her children, too. Your sister can still be wowed by a brother's unexpected thoughtfulness when he decides to buy her flowers. An aunt's wedding anniversary. To grandmother – just because. Your work colleague who's worked hard with you all week – any woman at any age on any given day will be gratified by your gift of flowers…

• Variety in flowers

There is never the same arrangement, the same color or the same kinds of flowers. All kinds of different varieties exist; even altered ones that are specially grown – like blue roses. Balloons with floral arrangements, candy tucked away in a bouquet, a little trinket hiding in the blooms. The diversity is endless. And so are the occasions for giving them. All kinds of different creative ideas of flowers for all different types of women in a man's life on the hundreds of special occasions as well as on ordinary days.

• Don't spend a fortune

It's true and everyone knows it, flowers, especially roses, double or even triple in price during extra special occasions, like Mother's Day or Valentine's Day. But it's the summer months that they are most in abundance and can be found, out of those special occasions, at far better value.

So, you can still get gorgeous bouquets done without having to pay a fortune, especially during the summer when there is far more variety.

- **Be impulsive**

Get your lady a trinket, a flower or any box of goodies out of the blue. Just because.

Not because it's her birthday, not because it's your anniversary and not because you had an argument and it's your way of saying sorry. All those times – giving a gift is almost mandatory.

But *do* act impulsively and get her a little something for no other reason than to let her know that you are thinking of her or you'd just like to demonstrate that you care.

It's the loveliest surprise for a woman – your spontaneity.

- **Get organized**

When you know exactly what gift you'd like to give a woman and you're about to either phone a catalog orders department or a florist or a gift store – there's nothing like stumbling at the beginning with doubts about correct delivery address, card message wording and even payment method.

So get yourself organized beforehand: who's the gift going to? Where is it to be delivered? Are you attaching a card? What message would you like to put on the card? When is it to be delivered? And your payment details ready on hand as well.

It doesn't take a lot of homework and it does save you a bit of time and trouble.

If you're still unsure about what to get her – it's a good time to ask the salesperson's opinion at this point. A little push in the right direction could be handy.

• Innovate

The first opportunity you get to try a different idea for a gift, go for it.

Nowadays, more and more people are breaking away from traditional gifts by adding some zest or innovative, creative hues to gifts that, from day to day, these ideas are being more and more appreciated.

Unusual, but tasteful, ideas for gifts, like champagne in a hot air balloon over beautiful country views or blue roses tinged with blue sparklies. Any gift that is an improvement on an old tradition is usually welcomed, especially as women are increasingly more aware of the different varieties being created all the time.

- **Ask the pros**

When in doubt, find it out; i.e., *ask*. Not the woman who you want to give the gift to, but the professional behind the counter, whether it's a make-up artist salesperson or an expert floral designer.

There are an increasing number of professional experts to guide you in good taste for the kind of woman you want to buy for. For example, a florist will be clued up on the personalized arrangement to suit the relationship status or woman's personality. So, go ahead and do ask for opinions and advice, it really might be the little flash of inspiration that failed you before.

- **An eternal gesture**

A woman's memory is usually quite long.

She'll remember the first gift you ever gave her. She'll remember the last gift you ever gave her. She'll even remember all the bouquets or single flowers you ever gave her.

It really does last longer in her memory.

So, all the more significant your gestures are of giving her a gift. All the times you give her a little something, fabulously huge or not – it will be quite eternal for her.

This last tip is to encourage you to go on ahead and give her gifts; whenever you can, she's sure to make it last.

HOW YOU CAN GO REALLY WRONG

I would rather trust a woman's instinct than a man's reason.

(Stanley Balwin)

You might not think it, but your gestures of gift giving might be getting you more into trouble than getting you into her good books. Or whatever other place you're trying to get into.

If you don't know her all that well or decide to get her the kinds of gifts that you think are great for you as well, well, you really might be looking at being totally single again.

This is what this guide is all about – getting you getting it right. So here are all the tips of all the things *not* to do. All the gifts *not* to give a woman. And how *not* to get your gifts returned or sold on eBay.

Typical gifts that are unwanted, undesirable and unwelcome are sports and outdoor equipment, bar accessories, car paraphernalia and entertaining stuff.

Women don't want to be given gifts that might add to their chores or give them extra work. Or seem as if it's a gadget to cut down on her chores.

The gift should really be for her luxury. Her feeling of relaxation or thrilling pampering.

Forget about beauty gifts you think will enhance her appearance. Or health items you think will help her or flatter her. These gifts are the ones that will shout out that you think she's either unattractive or unhealthy. *All* grave insults. So beware of these gift ideas.

The only exception to this rule is if she's actually asked you for these items for a gift or if you've been together long enough to be comfortable enough with her to get her these things, even if it's an electrical appliance that will help reduce her chores.

Still, don't make these kinds of gifts too customary.

Below, is a list to help you become the real hero in her eyes when you give her a gift. Pay attention. It's invaluable advice come from real experiences with real women.

A Woman's Worst Gifts:

Perfume

Any scent which is simply labeled 'Eau de toilet' or has a vaguely hidden name at the bottom of the bottle and was a really good bargain for you is a no-no. These so called colognes usually smell like a public toilet or a footballer's socks anyway.

If you're going to buy a woman a perfume, make sure you know her favorite brand or otherwise, buy her a good perfume or a well-known brand.

Women love perfume and usually they have a signature scent, when they don't, they're more flexible – they have a whole lot of varieties they like.

No woman will appreciate a cheap, no name brand for a perfume. Buying her one is one of the gravest mistakes you can make.

Even when you do buy her a gorgeously expensive perfume, if you're still unsure, keep the receipt and ask the salesperson if you can change it, before she actually opens the whole package. Tell her that you really want to splurge on something that she really likes and if she'd prefer another brand, then you can still change it.

Weight Loss

This is one much forbidden area to go into with women.

A gift certificate to weight Watchers or Jenny Craig might have you sleeping on the couch or lonesome single again.

You just *do not* give a gift like this to a woman.

Absolutely no gift that is associated to losing weight, getting fit or changing eating habits. No books on these, no DVDs, no accessories or equipment or programs or supplements. Nothing.

It's the worst insult to any woman. Especially a feminist.

If you offer a woman anything associated with dieting or weight loss or even exercising, you are telling her – really loudly – that you think she is fat. Or ugly. Or both. And that is one bad insult for women. You just simply do not go near these kinds of gifts.

The whole idea is to make her feel beautiful, sexy, attractive and that she's worth a million dollars.

These gifts will certainly never do that and if she never talks to you again, don't be surprised.

Bulk Gifts

Any gift that comes in jumbo size or 'buy 2 get 3' – is not a gift, especially as things that are sold on promotion like this are *usually* cleaning supplies.

And cleaning supplies are not gifts. They are actually never even given to a woman as a gift!

Even if you two have been in your relationship for years, you do *not* come home one day telling her what a great bargain you got and it should last her the rest of the year or so. That's like signing your death sentence.

Even if it isn't cleaning supplies, a gift that's bought in bulk and therefore means it will last and last demonstrates that a man is either a tightwad or so thrifty that he can't or won't buy a woman a luxury trinket which she'd really appreciate.

Women enjoy more intimate gifts or those that are decorative and contribute to her feeling of well being. Gifts in bulk don't do that. Avoid these.

Clothes

When you think that an item of clothing is an ideal gift for a woman, think again.

You might sincerely believe your taste in clothes is impeccable, after all, look at your own wardrobe. But it's a very tricky gift to give a woman.

You'll buy a woman an item of clothing, thinking how she would look good in it or thinking that she'd love you all the more for picking out something for her and… When you give it to her – well, she might smile and thank you; but don't be fooled.

There is no worse critic or colder analyst when it comes to women's clothing than the woman herself. Only *she* knows what looks good on her, what suits her and what makes her feel good.

And it is not any item of clothing you think looks sensational.

It is just the wisest choice to stay away from clothes as a gift for a woman.

She prefers picking out her own clothes, thank you.

She knows exactly what she wants and why she buys certain items – to match a pair of shoes or because her belt is the same shade.

Electrical appliances

No. Never. None. Not any.

No dishwasher, vacuum cleaner, blender nor infomercial multi-task miracle appliances that are meant to make housework a little easier. Housework goodies for a woman are *not* gifts. They smack of housewife duties and a gift is meant to have the opposite effect of taking away all reminders of housework.

Even feminine appliances are risky like hot curlers, blow driers or shaving appliances.

A woman likes to choose her own gadgets that will enhance her looks; she knows exactly which brands do the job better on her and which appliances to stay away from.

Although, if you are thinking of getting an electrical appliance, there are definitely better alternatives in naughty toys.

A woman won't mind if you buy her a toy that will enhance her well being in that sense, any toy that will contribute to her pleasure will be welcome. Just make sure that your relationship is on a comfortable level for this option, though *and* do your homework – find out what she likes and what she especially isn't fond of. Don't give her something that will shock or frighten her.

Imitation Jewelry

There is so much jewelry about imitating the real thing. The most common one being the infamous cubic zirconia passing off as diamonds.

This kind of gift is a lethal trap. If you're going to give your lady any kind of sparklies, you do *not* give the cubic zirconia kind or the emerald, ruby, sapphire *glass* kinds.

You give the real thing. Real diamonds or pearls. Real gold, whether it's white, yellow or pink. Stay away from anything that is gold plated anywhere.

She will find out if it's real or fake. Women are like that, you know. It's not that she'll run off to a jeweler to have her new trinket evaluated, although don't be surprised if she does, but she will probably plot a cruel revenge on you when she's showing off the rock you gave her to her friends by trying to cut glass with it and the *diamond* shatters.

She'll have the same reaction when the gold delicate chain you gave her starts discoloring or the pearl starts to peel off.

It is just bad taste to give fake jewelry.

Diamonds are not for everybody's budget.

So do invest in an authentic piece of sparkly decoration that is within your budget. The fact that it is real is already so well appreciated because it isn't the expense you had but the gesture you made that counts.

Kitchen Utensils

Any gorgeous collection of carving knives or any designer kitchenware, no matter how wildly fashionable, is *not* a feminine gift. It's just not a gift that will make a woman feel anywhere near special.

She may suspect that you're telling her something about cooking for you…

All kitchen utensils that are useful or practical are not recommended at all as gifts. No cookware, either. Something like this will contribute to her household duties again – just like the electrical appliances.

A woman wants a gift that pampers her. Something to take her away from the kitchen.

Besides, that set of knives can work against you one day, when she's really mad at you for going on a golfing vacation with all your golfing equipment sitting in the cupboard!

Flannels or Cartoons

Giving a woman lingerie is fine. In fact, it's one of the best gifts to receive.

But *never* if it's flannel.

Again, it's the practical idea behind the gift. The weather's cold – you'll give her a pair of flannel sleeping booties.

Or otherwise, you'll get her a nightshirt with all of Disney's princesses on it. She'll wonder if you're making any similarities to your kid sister…

It is both unflattering and insulting to give lingerie or underwear of any kind that is not made of lace, silk, satin or any other luxurious fabric.

Keep the flannels for the grandparents and the cartoon themes for the kids in the family.

A gift of lingerie should always be sexy. She wants to be sexy for you; she'll certainly appreciate a gift that smacks of sexiness. She'll *not* appreciate practical, cotton underwear for everyday use.

Gifts You Would Like

Another bad idea is to give a woman a gift that you would also like to have for yourself.

That is not a gift for her. It's a gift for yourself. Although you may argue that you'll both be able to use it and despite it being useful for her, it is also useful for you as well.

No. Don't even be tempted.

She'll see right through your intentions and know exactly that this gift was always intended for you rather than her.

Even if you're quite convincing that you were only thinking of her needs, she will still see it as something that suspiciously smells of chores and house work.

Again, it comes down to avoiding those functional gifts.

No matter how much you'd like that strimmer for the garden – you get her something exclusively for her use. Preferably feminine, too.

Feminists vs. Aging

And lastly, do not ever give women gifts that smack of females' bitchiness or a woman's wiles. And never give her any item for anti-aging.

There are thousands of gifts for the feminist today. But it isn't the sort of gift a man goes out and buys to give a woman. She won't appreciate the gesture and may start suspecting that you're telling her something indirectly.

Feminist t-shirts, posters or bags with witty remarks printed on them are not what a man gives as a gift. If she *is* a feminist, she'll buy her own brand of goodies with the messages she'll relate to. Not you.

Another thing you will not give her, unless you've decided you want out of the relationship, is any item that is for women's age reversal.

Stay away from anti-wrinkle creams or facial treatments. This is an insult to her looks as well as to how you regard her.

No matter how expensively lavish the cream or treatment, you give her things to pamper herself rather than try and take off a few years from her face!

BE UNPREDICTABLE!

A man chases a woman until she catches him.
                              (American Proverb)

There is nothing quite like the element of surprise. When a man turns around and does something so out of the ordinary, so unexpected, so *unpredictable,* the whole chain reaction is altered and so much more laughter and potential for reward comes swooping in.

Surprise really holds so much budding, latent joy; remember the feeling of arriving somewhere only to find it's your surprise party – the amazement of the unexpected. Or when you received a phone call from an old buddy you hadn't heard from in ages – what a good feeling from it having come as a surprise…

It is that element of unpredictability that changes everything from being mediocre to out of this world.

Using this knowledge can really make the woman in your life totally turn in your favor.

Women absolutely adore it when a man surprises her. When he does something she isn't expecting. Unpredictable gifts and unexpected surprises can melt the hardest heart of a woman.

According to Denise Lee, floral consultant and trend spotter from the Society of American Florists (SAF), the most unforgettable gifts for women are those men give unexpectedly. Very often, men buy flowers on special occasions, but it's when they do this out of the blue that it becomes magical.

For women, flowers coming as a gift when least expected, has the highest emotional impact and is the favorite way of receiving a gift: as a surprise!

Not only exclusively from a romantic partner, but anybody like a brother, son or colleague. But when it comes from a sweetheart, it comes far more welcomed. If it's a spontaneous gift, it's a wow gift and always so very good to receive.

According to Lee, flowers are typically the most successful gift given to women because they can say so much; they express love and romance, friendship and caring, gratitude and appreciation, congratulations and celebrations, apology and condolences. They are far from being given solely in the romantic context, but given from brother to sister, son to mother, employer to employee, friends and colleagues as well.

If a relationship is just about starting and you're still in doubt about giving a first spontaneous gift of flowers, don't be. Lee advises all men to go for it, not to think twice. The whole gesture of giving her flowers out of the blue is just so welcome and she will absolutely love it! You will feel like a million dollars as well.

The good thing about offering flowers is their *diversity*. Because there are hundreds of different types of flowers and bouquets, you can choose and be as varied as you like; you can certainly be as creative as you want with all the women in your life: different flowers for different relationships and to suit different personalities and moods.

The most popular flowers women love receiving are roses, says Lee.

She says that, firstly the flowers that always go when they're in high season, like Valentine's Day, are *roses*. They also go up in cost.

Secondly, the flowers used best to express a man's romantic feelings for a woman are *roses*. But they don't always have to be offered in high season. During the summer months they are much better value for money and they're in season all summer long, in abundance.

The majority of women also like *red* roses above other colors. A second close to this color are pastel shades. Many women are also quite fond of pale pinks, yellows, pearly and peach colors.

All women who love roses will especially enjoy a variety of colored roses, which, Lee says, is a spectacular gift that always succeeds in dazzling a woman. You don't always have to offer your sweetheart her favorite shade or favorite rose; there are also so many different types and varieties of roses as well.

Innovate.

Be creative.

Be unpredictable.

If the thought of having to go down to the florist and explaining the details of the bouquet of flowers you want to order puts you off, telling the florist why you want to send a bouquet, to who, the message you'd like to write and the quantity and quality of flowers can be quite intimidating.

But Lee suggests that if you're okay with leaving your car with the mechanic, you can also rely on the professionalism and discretion of a florist. They know what they're doing and you don't need to worry about any mishaps when placing your order for flowers.

It really is so much more worthwhile when that bouquet is offered spontaneously. Your sweetheart's bountiful reaction to your unexpected gift will be gratifyingly rewarding.

ON CHOCOLATES

I never met a chocolate I didn't like.

(Deanna Troi)

Chocolate…

Man's greatest rival.

Women even compare chocolate to sex and often it isn't men that come out the winners…

If you don't know it by now, the great majority of women and girls have quite a soft spot for chocolate.

Presenting a woman with a beautiful gift of chocolates can have her almost swooning at your feet. Chocolate has become so popular, so enjoyed, that major websites are making fantastic tributes to this food – and having more and more followers who like to contribute their ideas to these sites.

According to the American Fitness Association, almost half the female population in the U.S. is confirmed chocoholics! With one sixth of the male population admitting that they're real chocolate lovers as well.

Many of these chocolate lovers have said that chocolate has a soothing effect and just makes them feel good, all round.

There is even scientific research to back this up. Chocolate *does* make one feel good because it's been proven that it stimulates endorphins in the brain, which is the brain's natural anti-depressant chemical, producing a pleasurable feeling. These chemicals are also produced when a person is in love and there is this constant feel good sensation. Chocolate has the same effect; it really does make a person feel good, or at least temporarily euphoric.

Not only does it produce feelings of well-being, but a report in The Journal of the American Dietetic Association has also stated that chocolate is actually beneficial to our health. It's claimed that cocoa – dark chocolate, more specifically – contains flavonoids that decrease the chances of having cardiovascular disease. Also, it is an excellent source of antioxidants: the properties which help fight disease and prevent free radicals damaging our cells.

Dark chocolate is better and has more healthy properties than milk chocolate because of its higher cocoa content.

So, an excellent idea for a gift definitely is chocolate. The more expensive, the better the quality. A box of Belgian chocolates, truffles or even Hershey chocolates are all luxurious gifts and a woman's pleasure will be twofold when she unwraps that present and sees that you really did buy her one of her heart's truly desired pleasures.

It's a highly recommended gift.

Unless she has specifically told you that she's on a strict diet, then don't be too hasty with this type of gift. Or she's lactose intolerant – you might get away with dairy-free dark chocolate, in this instance.

Some advice on buying chocolate as a gift:

♦ Try and get a more expensive brand rather than an economical one. If they're a bit more costly, it's because they're really good quality chocolates. Also, with a good brand, it is quality that counts and not quantity; so, if you see a less expensive sort with more content, don't believe it's a better gift. Again, it's the mistake of buying in bulk.

More is not necessarily better.

Besides, she'll see what brand it is, probably know exactly how much those kinds of chocolates cost and she'll have a cooler reaction to your gift than you were expecting.

♦ Do your homework. Find out what she likes and doesn't like in chocolates. Although dark chocolate is a healthier option, not a lot of people like it because of its bitter taste. So, you won't offer a gift of dark chocolates if she isn't particularly fond of them.

Find out what kinds she likes, see what chocolate bars she'll eat and take it from there.

Normally, a chocolate lover will enjoy all chocolates, so a box of assorted chocolates with different fillings is a safe bet and she'll enjoy nearly all of them anyway.

♦ Go for attractive packages. Assorted kinds that are appealing to the eyes. Baskets with arrangements of chocolates. Unusual gift ideas for chocolates, here a salesperson's professional opinion will be handy. Or just a beautifully packaged box of luxury chocolates. The more attractive the presentation, the lovelier the gift and the more she'll be really pleased and grateful.

♦ Giving chocolate as a gift from your local supermarket or the store round the corner is a lovely gift. But imagine if those chocolates actually came from Belgium? Or Switzerland? Have you heard about Swiss chocolate or Belgian truffles? You don't have to bend over backwards to try and obtain exotic chocolates from real far-off chocolatiers.

Thanks to the internet, you can order these interestingly different chocolates from abroad – online. There are so many sites dedicated to chocolate, that most of them will have exquisite ranges to choose from as well as different chocolatiers to choose from.

...AND DIAMONDS

I have always felt a gift diamond shines so much better than one you buy for yourself.

(Mae West)

Nicole Kidman sang it 100% right in the film, *Moulin Rouge* – Diamonds are a girl's best friend…

They really are.

It isn't easy when you've buying your partner or other loved one gift for years; you've got it down to an art: you know all about flowers, chocolates, lingerie and yes, about all the female trimmings she likes.

But, so often, those gifts start making way into more functional gifts, practical goodies and even gifts better suited for the household and for the both of you rather than just for her. The romantic dinners start becoming more infrequent, the getaways start becoming family visits away and it all starts becoming predictable and comfortable. Well, for you at least.

It isn't always for her. The whole idea to keep the romance alive, to keep your relationship full of spark and to keep her very, very happy is *not* to continue on this path.

When the unexpected gift is jewelry, it has such a deep impact on her because it is a gift that will last for years to come and she can treasure it for its worth. In a recent survey, over half of the American female population said the best surprise gift they could ever receive was *jewelry*.

But while so many women claim they'd prefer jewelry, almost 60% of the male population said that they found buying jewelry for women stressful. And a quarter of these men had only a basic idea about what type of jewelry they'd buy for a woman!

Not only is it difficult to choose but they believe that in order to buy a woman a really attractive piece of jewelry, they'd have to cut into their budget.

There is also quite a lot of weight behind a gift like this and a lot of them believe that it would be too much pressure on them to offer a woman sparklies.

So, here are some tips to help you when it comes to purchasing a romantic gift of jewelry for the woman in your life. It is a guide only and meant to help get rid of any previous hesitancy on your part.

- On **wedding anniversaries**, giving the traditional anniversary gift is fine, paper on your 1st anniversary, cotton on your 2nd, etc. But it's a poor little gift and not that impressive or imaginative. At the beginning of a marriage when romance is still at its peak and romantic gifts still abundant, it is a very good idea to offer jewelry to a woman – she will never forget it. Ask her how she got her fine jewelry items – she will remember exactly who gave her which piece and even when; there's just that sentimental value to those items women have.

A woman doesn't forget who's given her these valuable gifts, so here's a good indicator as to how she'll react when you decide to give her a good quality trinket wrapped up in the traditional cotton or leather anniversary item.

Even if you've been married for years, she'll still remember every occasion you ever gave her jewelry.

• Giving flowers or candy on **Valentine's Day** is what is expected of all sweethearts. Why don't you do the unexpected, for a change as it's been advised earlier on in this book?

Giving an item of jewelry on this romantic day is the most romantic gift a man can offer a woman. And it'll be far more memorable and far more appreciated. As you both progress in your relationship, the more frequently you buy her jewelry, the more comfortable you'll become and you'll gain much more confidence in knowing what to get her because you'll be more familiar with her tastes. Practice does make perfect…

• One of the most memorable milestones in a woman's life – as well as the most romantic one – is the magical day of your **engagement** to each other. Naturally, here you will choose her ring with greater care as it is (supposedly) for life. It would be even more meaningful if you could take her somewhere special, in a romantic setting with all the trimmings for your engagement to be that bit extra special. It is the one occasion that she'll be talking about to friends and relatives for years to come. And she'll have her prized ring to show forever more.

• Make it **intimate**. The whole setting for you to give your lady love a piece of fine jewelry should be one that speaks directly and exclusively to her heart. Make it bigger for her; the whole experience of building up to it and then presenting her with the gift will make it all far more treasured and unforgettable for a lifetime. It doesn't take a great deal of talent or effort to offer her a gift with more trimmings, ideas and frills rather than just casually handing it over to her.

HOW DESPERATE ARE YOU?

Were there no women, men might live like Gods.
(Thomas Dekker)

So you are out to buy your lady a gift. And yet again that obscure quality has eluded you again: *inspiration.*

It is a hundredfold worse when it is those times of the year like Christmas or her birthday or your anniversary. It could even include all of your daughters and you got the task of buying the gifts.

Whichever scenario it is, it is daunting to say the least.

When a man has to know which perfect gift to buy his sweetheart, he'll wander the malls in search of that exact right gift that will light up her eyes but won't be too serious or reeking of commitment but not cheap goods, insensitive or cold or even a gift that will not appeal to her femininity.

It is a challenge to say the least. As to bearing the burden of having to buy for your daughters as well, I believe it is here that you hand over that responsibility to your wife, and rightly so.

It always seems that women have this 6th sense when it comes to gift giving. They always know what you need, want or love and their gifts always seem to be successful when they buy for their friends and relatives. Nature just didn't give men that intuitive blessing to men!

And so it becomes your worst nightmare when you are under duress to get her the gift of her dreams, especially if you're trying to win her over.

More often than not, those salespeople out there will see you for the desperado you're trying so hard not to be that they'll be able to sell you practically anything. You'll be a sitting duck. And you'll land up buying whatever trinket they so successfully talked you into buying that as you walk out the store, you suddenly get charged with major doubt and misgivings...

It wasn't bought out of inspiration, nor did you have a clue as to what she might need or would really like. You just bought it because the saleslady said it was what *all* women were buying that season.

Although you'll buy this lovely gift under pressure and seriously doubt the wisdom of that move, you'd be surprised at how much women actually do appreciate the gesture. Again, it comes down to the fact that you made the effort to run around looking for a gift just for her, there is some sentimental value to that. And although you probably gave her the latest, very popular scent going around in womandom, she just so happens to really dislike it.

But you got her something. And that makes it all worthwhile in her eyes.

Also, it deserves mentioning again because it cannot be said often enough – *do your homework.*

Pay attention – beforehand, of course – to the things she likes wearing, to her tastes in jewelry, to her favorite scents or even pampering bath items. It'll be a lot easier if you've heard her say lately how much she'd like a new CD or accessory for herself. Have you been listening lately? It makes your life oh-so much easier. And if you haven't picked up anything at all, then you start asking little innocent questions or make harmless suggestions to see what she says. You are bound to get more than one idea as what to get her.

You don't ask her directly what she'd like. That's insensitive and demonstrates lack of intelligence.

Never be fooled by a woman who says she doesn't want anything. If ever you ask what she'd like for Christmas and she says nothing – you'll be sleeping on that couch again if you really do give her nothing. You do not listen to a woman when this is ever said; it's the one time when she's saying no but doesn't really mean it. Not when it comes to gift giving.

Always buy her something, regardless of how small. And when you're going nuts because you don't know what to buy a woman who seems to have everything – take heart, go back and re-read the tips and advice given here. It's never that bad and you certainly don't have to resort to being a salesperson's victim simply because you didn't do your homework, didn't fish for information from her – or didn't read this book!

You've noticed that her sewing machine has packed up or that her tumble drier just worked for the last time ever after that suspicious bang. And her birthday happens to be coming up; you might think that you know exactly what you're going to get her. Inspiration was easy this time.

Wrong.

You'll be in real bad trouble if you're thinking of getting her a new tumble drier or sewing machine, no matter how badly she needs one.

These are items that smack of housework, hard work and just plain work. The whole idea is to give her a gift that will totally take her away from any kind of work. Be it house or no.

The kind of inspiration you need to get her an ideal birthday gift is the kind that will magically transform her into a grateful, appreciative and very happy woman: to pamper her, to give her a real treat, to be decorative or appeal to her senses.

Earlier in this book, you were told not to buy a woman clothes as a gift. This really is a wise tip.

But there are exceptions to this rule and as you're verging on getting desperate for a real worthwhile something and time is running out, here are some ideas that make it okay to offer an item of clothing to your sweetheart.

First of all, if you've been together for quite a few years, you already know her style and individual taste – well, at least some basic ideas by now – so it is safe, in this context, to get her an item of clothing she's had her eye on for a while. In fact, it's a really good idea to get her any clothing she's been wanting but is reluctant to get it herself.

Lingerie. Tasteful, feminine lingerie. This one will always be a winner. The more expensive the brand, the more appreciated it is. It isn't to say that you have to spend a fortune on a corset, just make it tasteful. And beautiful. Women *love* sexy, gorgeous lingerie. If you want to be bolder and go for the naughty kind of lingerie – make sure she likes it as well, or has suggested getting it for herself. Never give a woman lingerie that would be better suited for a woman walking the streets – that would be downright insulting. She might think you're sending out a less than appreciated message. Be careful with this one.

Moving away from expenditures and wandering the malls, looking for something for her – here's a very good idea to get her something she'll truly appreciate: your *time.*

Also, give her *time out* for herself.

In the busy, hectic world we live in, her responsibilities are twofold if she's a mom and there just isn't enough time to invest in your relationship anymore. Even if you two aren't living together – her career and social life might be just as demanding of her time.

So, plan an afternoon, evening or even a whole weekend away from familiar surroundings. Get away completely.

Go for a long walk on the beach, go sit and watch the sunset, go to the zoo for a day or another simple activity that you two can enjoy at leisure.

Once you do get to buy her a trinket instead – and one you hope to be the perfect gift she'll love, why not take it one step further and add a card?

It doesn't have to be a big one with really expressive poetic words where you just sign the bottom; it could be a small note or mini-card, one where *you* write your personal message.

It is a simple gesture – but it is so appreciated by womenfolk.

There's a good reason why she's kept all your old cards, notes and letters – women are really sentimental and keep all these things, with that *pink ribbon* wrapped round it and all.

Besides, *paper is patient.*

So, in that instant where you decide to write that note to her – that message will remain and she'll keep it for as long as she loves you.

The tricky part is what you'll write on that note. Some men are born writers and words just come easily to them, but others will have a tough time putting into words what they really feel. It isn't easy when you aren't a 'words' person.

Here's some straightforward advice: write something *simple.*

You don't have to research poems online or witty quotes, that's just too generic. Write something only the two of you relate to. Something sentimental. Tell her why you bought her that particular item, say that it reminds you of a romantic occasion in the past or refer it to her attractiveness in your eyes.

Make it personal.

And if you're one of the lucky ones who does have a flair for words – make it sincere. She'll know exactly when it isn't genuine nor about anything especially intimate about herself or the two of you.

It's the most treasured kind, when it comes straight from the heart and it will hold so much more sentimental value in the years to come when she'll add it to her pink ribboned others.

So, you are now armed with more useful information than before you picked up this book. You cannot go wrong now; unless you fall into old habits of venturing into the general gifts aisle or stores. There you'll become mediocre – or less – in her eyes because you got her any old gift. If you're okay with this, then you'll have to be okay when she gives you the cold shoulder and you wonder what you did wrong and *when*?

A FEW REALLY GOOD IDEAS

I really think that American gentlemen are the best after all, because kissing your hand may make you feel very good but a diamond and sapphire bracelet lasts forever.

(Anita Loos)

When you've decided that you're going to invest in a really worthwhile gift such as a piece of jewelry, you know you can't go wrong because fine jewelry is always appreciated and costly. You are right.

But when you notice that she doesn't wear that item, hardly ever or even at all – you're left wondering why? It was a gorgeous piece. It was not that cheap nor that mediocre – in your opinion, at least.

In this scenario, the problem isn't your taste. It's hers.

You bought her a truly lovely gift that doesn't either suit her style or her taste. Or it was the kind of gift she'd probably buy for her chiwawa…

You haven't been paying attention, really *looking* at her. What have you noticed about the jewelry she wears? Judging by her taste, her style in what she already wears should already point you in the right direction of exactly what styles to buy for her.

If she wears bold jewelry, buy her bigger baubles.

If she wears fine, delicate jewelry, buy her delicate, feminine items.

If she doesn't wear any jewelry, find out first if

her ears are pierced before you choose a pair of earrings; fish for information if she's allergic to silver or only really likes yellow gold.

And then buy her classic jewelry which is suitable for everyday use as well as evening wear.

But you have to pay attention or do some kind of investigative work like asking her sister or friend about her tastes.

After you've made a mental note (or actual physical one) of her taste in jewelry, her style and what she especially wouldn't appreciate; then it's safe to get to that jeweler's and make your selection from there.

This is your homework done:

Her favorite metal: yellow or white gold or platinum?

With any stones? If so, which are her favorite? Better yet, which ones does she not like?

Pierced earrings? Other kinds of body piercings? Which ones?

Chains, bracelets and rings: are they bulky and big; flashy and heavy? Or are they tiny and delicate, feminine and discreet?

Does she wear or even have any jewelry ensembles? I.e. numerous items of jewelry that all match? Or just the odd piece she wears occasionally?

All this will guide you in buying her a gift she'll not only wear proudly and show off to everyone around her but she'll treasure and keep for a very, very long time.

All things considered, you can't exactly be buying jewelry every other day and as frequent spontaneous gifts; there are loads of other feminine gifts to surprise her with and to keep her guessing as well as very much in love with you for demonstrating how much you care and are thinking of her with these gifts of yours.

So what other kinds of baubles can you give a woman that she'll really want? The ideas are endless and here are the main ones that the majority of women will appreciate.

Any gift that's for good for pampering: bubble bath, bath oils, shower gels, body lotions, fragrances, massage oils, perfume sets with a whole range of body lotions, talc and body scrubs included. All of these are delicious goodies any woman enjoys – you're catering to her indulgence and treating her to real luxuriant, relaxing experience. Depending on your budget, an alternative would be to purchase a health spa experience day, where she gets treated to a full body massage, fitness workout, sauna and maybe a facial as well.

Although with the home version, you can share the experience with her, indulge her better and make it far more intimate.

Any item of lingerie. Note: tasteful, feminine, sexy lingerie. Preferably *comfortable* as well.

Usually the lovelier and more feminine pieces are not the ones you'll find so easily – it takes some looking around for superior brands that have quality over quantity. Whether it's at the mall or online, brands such as Gossard, Warner and Rigby & Peller, to name a few, are some of the best brands you can look into, although you must be willing to cut into your budget somewhat – a really good item of lingerie can last her a lifetime because of enduring quality, or as long as she fits into it.

It's imperative to stress that if you're going to buy her lingerie, buy it exclusively for her and not because you'd like to see her in leather-look-alike plastic garter belts and corset, this kind of lingerie is mainly for you and while she might not mind that, remember you should be giving her a gift to last and that suits her tastes. And one she'll appreciate longer.

If she is into the whole green movement of saving the planet; a gift you could consider is giving her the opportunity to adopt an animal. This is one of the kindest gesture you could make and people who are Earth conscious feel that all these acts of kindness are making all the difference. A gift like this would be ideal for her and you would get to prove how sensitive and caring you are to the same issues that she's concerned about.

So, go online and look for organizations, like WWF, there's an abundance of opportunities for this kind of gift; her reaction to this offering of yours would be beyond gratifying.

Romantic gifts have always got a powerful sway in a relationship. So, for a change, instead of going for lingerie or the pampering goodies, use your imagination and get her something really syrupy-sweet. A romantic gift could be anything between a flower canvas portrait which has been personalized with a special message from you to her right up to a book on love poems, with a collection of major works on love, written with a personal message again.

Cooking dinner for her, turning down the lights, lighting the candles, putting on her favorite ballads playing softly in the background, pulling out her chair for her to sit then serving her dinner – *this* is romance!

Food, in its luxurious form, has always been offered as gifts. It was a welcoming gesture to offer food like a pie or cookies when a new neighbor moved into the neighborhood. But not just any food put together, usually the sweet kind. A hugely successful gift that is still enormously popular today is the food hamper, wine hamper, chocolate hamper, well, you name it – it exists.

During festive seasons they're more abundant, but you'll find them online as well as stores who specialize in hampers.

It is a lovely gift to give to a woman of any age, all candy and chocolates are excellent choices. Sometimes, the creativity that goes into this gift helps take the burden off your shoulders by having to get creative yourself. But take this sort of gift one step further – personalize it.

If it's a viable option, get her name printed on some of the candy boxes, otherwise both of your names or a small message for her printed on some wrappers.

She'll be so thrilled that she'll keep those wrappers along with all the other cards in that ribboned stack for years to come.

SPECIAL OCCASIONS

Women deserve to have more than twelve years between the ages of twenty-eight and forty.

(James Thurber)

A special occasion is that day of the year when a woman knows she'll be esteemed by the physical demonstration of your consideration in the form of presenting her with a 'little something.'

And there are enough of those occasions to fill the whole calendar, which should keep you on your toes until you're really practiced in the art of gift giving. When it isn't the annual festive occasions like Christmas and Easter, it'll be Valentine's Day or International Women's Day. Then, there's Mother's Day, Girlfriend's Day and even Mother-in-Law's Day.

And then, there are all the 'just because' days when you're being your usual unpredictable self and getting her trinkets out of the blue to surprise her and keep the romance alive in your relationship.

For some of those occasions, here are gift suggestions as well further tips to guide you.

Gift Ideas for Mother's Day

This is the one day of the year that moms should really have time off for themselves or to enjoy the company of their loved ones and *really* get spoilt.

Firstly, because she really deserves it and secondly, not surprisingly, she really appreciates the attention and the pampering on this day.

It's obvious that when choosing a gift for her, you aren't going to get her any old thing that you think she needs or would probably find useful around the house. Also, it isn't very wise in assuming that an ideal gift for her on Mother's Day is also one that dad can use.

Getting mom a gift should require the same kind of investigative work you'd do for your sweetheart, the same kind of careful planning and paying attention to what mom would enjoy.

The only difference from your sweetheart would probably be the desire to spend her quality time with her whole family – whereas your partner would prefer an intimate getaway just for the two of you.

Getting mom some time away from the family might be exactly what she needs and she would probably enjoy that the most; so perhaps a reservation at a good restaurant with dad or her partner in life would be deeply appreciated.

On the other hand, perhaps a planned day's outing with the family and all those she holds dear would suit her better, maybe she doesn't get the opportunity to share so much time with these people and this gesture would please her tremendously.

Most moms would enjoy time spent with all her loved ones, especially when they're all set to spoil and pamper her.

As for gifts, when mom's have already got grandchildren, or still have small children of their own - one of the most cherished gifts they could receive are little crafted items done by the children and given as a gift. This kind of gift will surely be appreciated as it will hold sentimental value for life, long after the children have grown up.

It is also still very traditional to give mom flowers on this day – if you're going to opt for this alternative – be sure to make it as personal as you can. Include a personalized small bottle of champagne in the bouquet with her name and a personal message printed on the bottle or a hand written card with your special message.

Even offer to have the bouquet dried afterwards and she can keep it much longer as a memento.

Instead of flowers, give her jewelry. The kind that suits her individual taste, regardless of her age. It is another gift that will last for a long time she'll attach sentimental value to. She definitely won't ever forget who it came from and when; but that's all women for you.

Another gift that mom might really enjoy is a pampering health spa day away just for herself. Although it is always wisest to be sure if she would enjoy this kind of gift, especially on Mother's Day. Some moms who are very active in their careers and family rearing might choose this kind of getaway simply because it's something they wouldn't get for themselves and probably don't get it offered often. Or ever.

So, it really depends on mom's lifestyle and it definitely depends on her tastes and if she's ever expressed any desire to get away as a treat.

All things considered, mom is still all woman. And just because she's older and wiser and has many more years experience of life, doesn't mean that she'll be impressed with *everything* she gets given as a gift.

Y   ou can still get it wrong when you offer her a gift that *you* think is appropriate for her.

The very worst thing that could happen is you

forgetting Mother's Day. Cardinal sin, this. So, if you are the forgetful kind or just have too much going on in your life, you make a *point* of keeping this day as a permanent reminder on your laptop calendar or have a secretary remind you. If you're a son, it's deeply wounding should you ever forget this day. So, *don't.*

It has been mentioned earlier on in this book – you never give a woman electrical appliances or any electrical items for housework; either because they're practical or because you think mom needs or deserves a functional little gadget to make her life easier.

Just because she's a mother does not make her an exception to this rule.

As a woman, she doesn't want anything remotely associated to work, practical housework or house functionality.

Besides, doesn't she deserve the same kind of pampering and spoiling as your partner does? Maybe even more so.

If you're really all out of ideas as to what to get her – she seems to have everything and doesn't need any more bric-a-brac lying around the house – you can ask her; more than likely she'll tell you she doesn't want anything and she certainly doesn't need anything.

Don't take this answer to heart.

No matter how she may insist on not wanting anything and she'd be quite satisfied with your company – you do *not* get her nothing.

When Mother's Day comes around and you arrive there with really nothing, it will still be disappointing for her – somewhere in her – it really will.

So, really *do* turn a deaf ear on her when she says 'nothing' and you go and buy her a nice, heartwarming gift. And this gesture, this gift on this special day *will* gladden her heart: because you made the effort. Definitely deeply gratifying.

Gift Ideas for Anniversaries

For every year that you celebrate your anniversary, there is a traditional item, usually a source of material, which is typically given to one another or other celebrating couples – like cotton, steel, glass, etc.

But more contemporary alternatives have emerged, not to substitute the traditional ideas completely, but to complement them – also in keeping with the ever changing consumerism.

Below is a chart of anniversary gifts usually given, both the traditional and modern.

Anniversary Year	Traditional	Modern
1st	paper	plastic/ clocks
2nd	cotton	china
3rd	leather	crystal / glass
4th	flowers	linen / nylon / silk
5th	wood	silverware
6th	candy	iron / wood
7th	copper / wool	copper / wool /brass
8th	bronze / pottery	bronze / linen / lace
9th	pottery / china	pottery / willow / leather
10th	Tin / aluminum	diamond
11th	steel	fashion jewelry
12th	silk	linen / pearl
13th	lace	textile / fur
14th	ivory	gold jewelry
15th	crystal glass	watches
20th	china	platinum
25th	silver	silver
30th	pearl	pearl
35th	coral / jade	jade
40th	ruby	ruby
45th	sapphire	sapphire
50th	gold	gold
60th	diamond	diamond

Appendix

Birthstones

An inspired gift you can give a woman is her personal birthstone, which is a gemstone associated with each calendar month. Her birthstone can be given in a ring, bracelet, a solitaire on a chain or even in stud earrings; whichever item of jewelry you choose, she's bound to be impressed that you knew which was her birthday gem.

You'll find that most women know what their birthstone is because of the mysterious past of these birthstones.

It was believed that each astrological sign had its own precious or semi-precious stone associated to it and as far back as 1400 BC, the Assyrians attributed magical properties to these stones. Each stone had its own power, even for healing and it was believed that wearing these stones against the skin, according to your astrological sign, would bring you good luck, have healing properties and even enhance feelings of well-being.

Much of this is still believed today and semi-precious stones are being used now more than ever in alternative healing therapies.

There were various stones attributed to each month and too many civilizations had their own versions: the Russians had one criterion, the Polish another, the Romans yet another list for birthstones and so on. The American National Association of Jewelers, today known as The Jewelers of America, adopted one single list of birthstones for each month of the year in 1912.

The following are all the birthstones associated with their respective months of the year. Some months have more than one birthstone but these are the most common ones found today.

January: Garnet

When we talk about the garnet, the majority of people think this stone is a deep red color, but it is a gem that comes in different tones except blue. Other brilliant color garnets are the orange Malaya garnet, the pink rhodolite garnet, the green tsavorite garnet and in Arizona, there are the bright red anthill garnets.

So, you don't have to think you're offering her a red stone when she doesn't favor the color red much; you can go for other hues in garnets and still offer her the right birthstone. Also, you can offer her a more expensive stone by buying her a rarer stone or a more affordable garnet, for they are varied in price range.

Garnets are believed to help fight blood deficiencies, increase sexual drive, gain courage and fight depression.

February: Amethyst

This gemstone is more abundant and more easily available. An amethyst ranges from light lilac all the way to deep purple hues.

Royalty has always favored this gemstone as it has always favored the color purple, so it will very often be found in royal crown jewels and in ancient Greek and Egyptian adornments.

Amethyst is reputed to prevent and help against drunkenness and inebriation and is said to have a sobering effect when worn on the skin. It's said to help tone down strong, passionate emotions and aid the psychic. Desirable characteristics. If you know this information, you can always impart with it to your lady love and it can certainly make this birthstone that much more valuable to her.

March: Aquamarine

Typical tones of this gem are pale blues, usually clear pale sea blue, greenish-ble and even a deeper blue. Some aquamarines may be smoky with gray or green hues but the superior gem will be clear; the rarer gems will be the darker ones. When this stone is a larger cut, whether oval or squarish, it tends to have an enhanced sparkle which makes it far more attracting than a smaller sized aquamarine.

It was believed that this stone had magical properties to protect those who traveled the waters. Centuries ago, sailors would carry this gemstone on their ships to aid in their voyages – today it's believed to aid against sea sickness.

It is also claimed that those who wear this gemstone attract affectionate love and new friends; it also helps ease tensions between couples as it's supposed to have a soothing effect.

April: Diamond

A colorless gem this precious stone also exists in transparent yellow, green, purple, pink, red and grey.

A clear, flawless stone is the most sparkly and most expensive one of all. Unfortunately, so many sparklies exist to imitate this brilliant one – when you do buy one, make sure you aren't buying synthetic moissianite or a colorless sapphire.

This stone really is the gift of love. As well as being a long lasting token of love, the diamond is believed to help memory improvement and concentration. It was believed that a diamond would reflect the health of the person wearing this stone, if health was poor, the diamond would lose its brilliance but when the wearer was in good health again, the diamond would be all sparkly again.

May: Emerald

This green gemstone is usually clear with some greens having yellowy or bluish hues. Its deep shades of dazzling green are attractive on any person and it is a beautiful gift which almost rivals the diamond. *Almost.*

As it is a color associated with serenity, it's the perfect stone to wear against the skin for a calming effect.

It was claimed that the emerald would attract good luck, increase wisdom, possesses amazing healing powers and helps against mental and emotional illnesses. It was even said that the stone would change color in the presence of false friends or liars and enhanced the ability to see the future.

June: Pearl

Unlike other gemstones that come from the Earth, this one comes from water – especially oysters and clams, where it will be built up slowly by the mollusk. The traditional pearl is usually rounded or elongated and commonly white or black. But you can find pearls that are gray, blue, yellow and lilac. Rarely, pink – these are the most prized pearls.

They are supposed to be emotionally stabilizing and help heal problems with the stomach, spleen and ulcers as well.

It was also believed that when worn against the skin, pearls could enhance self-esteem, happiness, love and success. Pearls have also been associated to chastity and modesty.

Share this knowledge with your sweetheart when you get her any pearly pieces and see her eyes glow! Well, maybe not about the chastity part.

July: Ruby

A deep crimson red stone – the ruby is not as abundant as other gemstones and not as economical either. It's rare to find a bigger sized ruby as very often they're naturally small stones.

This stone symbolizes love, power, passion, vitality and success; it is believed to be an energizing gem that promotes success and confidence in the person wearing it.

In history, it was the most prized gemstone in that only royalty of the very highest possessed this stone; it was believed to attract wealth, health and power.

Rubies are claimed to detoxify the blood, lower fevers, improve the circulatory system and are good for the heart when worn on that area.

Because this gem carries so much vitality and vibrant energy – it is the perfect gift to demonstrate your passionate feelings and deep love.

August: Peridot

A green stone that ranges from pale green, yellowish green and an olive green, it is also known as precious olivine. It's more accessible and costs about the same as a garnet and tourmaline.

In ancient times, Peridot was worn to aid foresight and the arts of divinity; it was a gemstone favored by royalty, even some of Cleopatra's emeralds were peridots.

Believed to help increase physical strength, it was also used to attract prosperity as well as love, temper down all rages and angry emotions and help sleep at night.

A beautiful, sparkly stone for women born in August, it has such a favorable reputation in history that your sweetheart would not take this gem off.

September: Sapphire

This gemstone is typically blue, a deep blue; but they also exist in other colors, orange, violet, pink, green and even black sapphires as well as the colorless sapphire which looks like a diamond. These colored sapphires are not as costly as the typical blue one because the stone is purer and more velvety in shine.

The sapphire was believed to ward off illness and negativity and also to offer protection; it was used in sorcery to give sight into the astral plane and protect them against evil.

It went so far as to be believed that the stone could be used as a communicator with the Universe, angels and spirit guides.

So, this gorgeous stone will certainly be a boon to the woman whose birthday is in September. You can tell her truthfully that wearing this stone against her skin will offer her protection, serenity and promote positivity.

October: Opal

This gemstone can be found in about three or four colors: the most common ones being a milky shade of white – with flashing, fiery hues in it of green, orange, blue and pink and the fire opals which are yellow, orange or red. The rarer one is a darker shade of dark gray, dark blue and black, also with flashing hues of red, blue and purple in them.

All three colored opals have reputed healing properties and in the Middle ages, opals were used for different bodily disorders – the white opal was used for neurological problems, the fire opal for depression and blood disorders and the rarer black opal was especially beneficial for problems associated with the reproductive organs and sexuality; this black one was also considered a powerfully lucky charm. It is still believed today that the opal is associated to desire and eroticism – not a bad thing to tell your lady love when you give it to her. It's one of the prettiest gemstones to offer as a gift because of the different colors it reflects, the bits of brilliant rainbows in it.

November: Topaz

A blue or gold hued stone yes, but topaz exists in many other colors: green, yellow, brown and the rarer shades of red and deep pink. Some topazes are even heated through to become pink. Colorless topazes look just like diamonds - sparkle, shine and all. In fact, if you're on a budget and would like to give a diamond, this is a good imitation of one. Perhaps not a good idea to tell her it *is* a diamond, though.

Topazes are believed to help against bleeding and blood disorders, it was given to promote strength, calm, serenity and to tranquilize stronger passions. Even putting a topaz under one's pillow at night is thought to ward off nightmares and give a peaceful night's sleep.

As a gift of strength – it is bound to please your sweetheart as all women feel they could do with this sort of gift at any time of their lives.

December: Turquoise

This stone is not a clear one like other gemstones but opaque, with little veins or darker lines; it's the exact color of its name: turquoise – a bright sky blue, although they're also found in shades of greenish blue, yellow and gray.

It's a great gift of happiness and good fortune – believed to attract healing spirits; it was considered a powerfully protective and healing stone.

It's not costly, quite abundant and can even be carved or engraved if you'd like to give a gift that was shaped or with your sweetheart's name's initial. It is particularly beautiful when it is set in gold or other precious metals, so if you'd like to give her something more valuable, you can go for this setting or another valuable stone to either complement or contrast with turquoise. You can even inform her that early native

Americans as well as Egyptians wore this stone as significant decorative jewelry.

Ring Size Chart

When you don't know the ring size for the woman who you'd like to buy a ring for, this chart will help you get the right size, if you can get to that finger without her realizing it!

1 - Wind a piece of string or chord loosely around the base of the finger.

2 - Mark the spot on the string that overlaps with a pen.

3 - Measure the length of this string that you winded round the finger.

4 – Use the measurement to find the correct size in the following chart:

Measured Size		Ring Size
inches	**mm**	USA
1.8307	46.5	4
1.8818	47.8	4.5
1.9291	49.0	5
1.9803	50.3	5.5
2.0275	51.5	6
2.0787	52.8	6.5
2.1259	54.0	7
2.1771	55.3	7.5
2.2283	56.6	8
2.2755	57.8	8.5
2.3267	59.1	9
2.3740	60.3	9.5
2.4251	61.6	10
2.4724	62.8	10.5
2.5236	64.1	11
2.5708	65.3	11.5
2.6220	66.6	12

LOVE POEMS

If Galileo had said in verse that the world moved, the inquisition might have let him alone.
(Thomas Hardy)

You do not have to be good at poetry, prose or writing to be able to pen a small, simple note to a loved one.

The reason why you should at least write a note is when you're going to *personalize* a gift to her, then you get her a pretty card or just a small message note and you write her a message which is just from you.

A personal message that is romantic, that expresses your reason for buying her that gift on that day, how you feeling about her at that moment, the reasons why you want to stay with her or just to say why you love her.

But some men are really hard pressed to say more than 'I love you' and well, even that is sometimes not all that you'd like to say.

You can search online for love poems because there are millions of poems to suit every occasion, every woman and every relationship you have with all the different women in your life.

Only – *never* copy somebody else's poem (regardless of how obscure that somebody is) and tell her you made it up; no matter how much you really are tempted into taking the credit for it – *don't*.

You might never get found out, but do you want to get caught lying?

Where To Buy This Book

You can buy this book on Amazon. Just go to amazon.com (or your local Amazon site if available) and search for "Best Gift Ideas For Women by Taylor Timms" or "Taylor Timms".

You can also order it at any bookstore if they don't have it in stock. Just give them the IBSN below:

ISBN 978-0-9866004-4-9